NONE

DARE

CALL

IT

TREASON!

BOOK 12

Wholesale Treason
During the War
In Vietnam!

Robert W. Pelton
$4.95

"Treason doth never prosper,

"What's the reason?

"Why if it prosper,

"None dare call it treason."

John Harrington

Printed in America
On Recycled Paper
In
Charleston, South Carolina

Published in America
By
The Freedom & Liberty
Foundation Press
Knoxville, Tennessee

Dedicated
To

The greatest, most generous, most benevolent and most powerful nation on the face of the earth – and the only country in the history of the world to have been founded on Biblical principles.

A nation can survive its fools, and even the ambitious. But it cannot survive treason from within.

An enemy at the gates is less formidable, for he is known and he carries his banners openly.

The traitor moves among those within the gates freely, his sly whispers rustling through the galleys, heard in the very hall of government itself.

For the traitor appears not traitor. He speaks in the accent familiar to his victims, and he wears their face and their garments, and he appeals to the baseness that lies deep in the hearts of all men.

He rots the soul of a nation - he works secretly and unknown in the night to undermine the pillars of a city - he infects the body politic so that it can no longer resist.

A murderer is less to be feared.

Cicero, 42 B.C.

CONTENTS

Dedication   7

Forward   13

Preface   17

Wholesale Treason
      During the War
         In Vietnam!   27

Epilogue   103

    Other Books of Interest
         By This Author   109

Meet the Author   117

Forward

**Independence Hall Where the Declaration
of Independence Was Signed.**

Our glorious Declaration of Independence is a timeless divinely inspired masterpiece given to mankind through the anointed pen of Thomas Jefferson.

The grand and unmatched United States Constitution is indisputably the product of Providential guidance and wisdom and certainly not a document which evokes whimsical interpretations with the changing political climates.

All Americans have a moral obligation to stand up and be counted in these trying times!

Abraham Lincoln boldly declared: *"To sin by silence when they should protest, makes cowards of men."*

William Lloyd Garrison capsulized it best: *"As a free man who is determined to remain free -- I do not wish to think or speak, or write with moderation. "Tell a man whose house is on fire to give a moderate alarm; tell him to moderately rescue his wife from the hands of a ravisher; tell the mother to gradually extricate her babe from the fire into which it has fallen -- but urge me not to use moderation in a course like the present."*

Senator Barry Goldwater, 1964 Presidential candidate was castigated and verbally crucified by the media.

He simply stated this simple truism: *"Extremism in the pursuit of Liberty is no vice."*

This good and moral man of character soundly rocked the boat of the propagandists. He was as a result soundly defeated in the election.

The alarmed media wolves panicked the voters with their jeers and sneers and insane howls about this man's lack of *"moderation!"*

It can honestly be said that through the Providential genius of our Founding Fathers, the remaining remnants of the original American Constitutional Republic still provides more freedom, opportunity and abundance for mankind than is found in any other nation in the world.

This is true despite decade after decade of unabated treason and treachery promulgated by innumerable traitorous individuals found buried in the twiddle dee – twiddle dum administrations of both the Democrats and the Republicans.

 An informed and active, not a media brainwashed electorate, is the only antidote to further prostitution of, and the ultimate destruction of, what Benjamin Franklin called our Republic.

Preface

"Treason against the United States shall consist only in levying war against them, or in adhering to their enemies, giving them aid and comfort."

U.S. Constitution. Article 111, Section 3

What is your treason I.Q.?

If you can answer the following questions, it's high.

If you miss one or more, you should read the *None Dare Call It Treason* series!

Who was behind allowing Red Chinese soldiers take airborne training at Fort Benning, Georgia?

Is this not treason?

Why was South Vietnam, South Africa, Rhodesia and numerous other American friends deliberately betrayed to the forces of evil?

Is this not treason?

Why was our friend Chiang Kai Shek not so gently coerced into a Communist dictatorship by highly placed subversives in the State Department?

Is this not treason?

Why was Cuba treasonously delivered into the clutches of Communist revolutionary Fidel Castro?

Is this not treason?

Why have untold millions of dollars consistently been used to prop up faltering Red dictatorships and to assist Communist terrorists in overthrowing non-Communist governments?

Is this not treason?

What American company sold nuclear reactors to Communist Occupied Romania?

Is this not treason?

Name the company that provided Communist Hungary with a factory designed to make 1.5 million light bulbs daily?

Is this not treason?

What well known oil company invested $1 billion for oil exploration in Communist Occupied Angola?

Is this not treason?

Can you name the American company who treasonously built and equipped a $10 million electronics plant near Warsaw for the Polish slave labor tyranny?

Is this not treason?

These are questions to which every American should rightfully have an honest answer.

Unfortunately most do not!

Tragedy was carefully orchestrated by traitors in our Government and the media with regard to Cuba, Vietnam, Laos, Cambodia, Rhodesia, China, El Salvador, Nicaragua and many other countries. Anastasio Somoza was the former President of free Nicaragua.

He offered this startling insight in his 1980 book, Nicaragua Betrayed: *"I have factual evidence that the betrayal of Nicaragua was not perpetrated out of ignorance, but rather by design."*

Somoza was soon after assassinated!

Is this not treason?

John Lehman, Secretary of the Navy, made this shocking statement on May 25 to the 1983 Annapolis graduating class: *"Within weeks many of you will be looking across just hundreds of feet of water at some of the most modern technology ever invented in America.*

"Unfortunately, it is on Soviet ships."

Is this not treason?

Earl E.T. Smith was the American Ambassador to Cuba when it was similarly delivered to the Communists.

He makes this concise comment on July 14, 1986: *"Nicaragua is Cuba all over again."*

Can you name the company that paid the Communist dictatorship in Angola over $600 million annually in taxes and oil royalties.

This money bought new Soviet jets, tanks and helicopter gunships.

And it paid Castro for supplying 35,000 imported Cuban mercenaries who keep the Angolan people enslaved.

Is this not treason?

Stressed retired Brigadier General Andrew J. Gatsis on August 11, 1986: *"Though aware of the Communist goal of world domination, the average U.S. Citizen refuses to believe that the real threat comes from governmental officials and their non-governmental confederates who secretly espouse the same objectives as the openly avowed Communists."*

Anthony Sutton stated in his 1986 book *The Best Enemy Money Can Buy: "We now have the formidable task of bringing these gentlemen to the bar of justice to publicly answer for their private and*

concealed actions."

The *None Dare Call It Treason* series certainly won't win accolades from the United Nations or the State Department!

Nor will Harvard feel compelled to bestow an honorary degree upon the author!

Harvard Law School was the spawning ground for an incredible number of Red agents. Included were members of the first Soviet spy ring ever to be exposed in our government.

Reed Irvine aptly commented in July of 1986: *"Indeed, it has long been a joke among refugees from Eastern Europe that there are more Marxists at Harvard than there are in the Soviet Union, or Poland, or whatever Communist country the refugee called home."*

The Honorable Ezra Taft Benson said: *"The truth must be told even at the risk of destroying, in large measure, the influence of men who are widely respected and loved by the American people.*

"The stakes are high. Freedom and survival is the issue."

Treason is still a most serious federal offense.

The *None Dare Call It Treason* series examines the reasons for and the Americans behind the fall of freedom and the rise of tyranny throughout the world!

Has anything really changed?
You Decide!

Treason

Whoever, owing allegiance to the United States, levies war against them or adheres to their enemies, giving them aid and comfort within the United States or elsewhere, is guilty of treason and shall suffer death, or be imprisoned not less than five years and fined not less than $10,000; and shall be incapable of holding any office under the United states.

U.S. Code, Title 18, Section 2381

Whoever, owing allegiance to the United States and having knowledge of the commission of any treason against them, conceals and does not, as soon as may be, disclose and make known the same to the President or to some judge of the United States, or to the Governor or to some judge or justice of a particular state, is guilty of misprision of treason, and shall be fined not more than $1000 or imprisoned not more than 7 years or both.

U.S. Code, Title 18, Section 2382

Wholesale Treason During the War In Vietnam

Treason: *"Betrayal of one's country to an enemy."*

Webster's New World Dictionary

Americans were fighting and dying in a tragic no-win War in Vietnam.

Communist Occupied China was supplying our North Vietnamese enemy with light weapons, military equipment, at least 4,000 battle hardened officers and 320,000 combat veterans!

Yet a Georgia newspaper headline revealed this shocker: **"RED CHINESE SOLDIERS TO TRAIN AT FORT BENNING."**

Yes, Americans were ordered to train the soldiers of a deadly Communist adversary they were already facing in battle during the Vietnam War!

Who could possibly have approved such leftist lunacy?

A nameless and faceless Defense Department spokesman offered a ludicrous rationalization for training soldiers from Communist Occupied China.

He said: *"The United States*

Government now regards China as a 'friendly, non-allied' country.

"This policy is based upon the assessment that a modernizing, more secure China which shares with the United States a common threat [the Soviet Union] can be an increasing force for peace and stability in East Asia [As China has been in Cambodia, Vietnam, Tibet, Korea, etc.?]."

Strangely enough, the Department of Defense still secretly listed Communist Occupied China as *"hostile to the United States"*.

This was the same lame excuse used years ago by leftists regarding Communist Occupied Russia.

Americans were then told the snarling Russian Bear must be aided and appeased to make it *"feel more secure."*

The Soviets had to be fed and armed because *"a common threat"* was shared.

At that time the *"common threat"* was supposedly Communist Occupied China.

Suffice to say, Communist Occupied Russia saw fit in 1985 to sign a very friendly $14 billion trade agreement with America's new found Red Chinese *"ally"*.

Marine Lieutenant Robert G. LoPresti had to use worn-out equipment in a field hospital near Pleiku.

Spare parts weren't available for the generators at the field hospitals.

Nor was the proper medical equipment!

Wounded marines died unnecessarily as a result.

Upon returning to the United States, LoPresti found the Communists were being supplied massive quantities of the same spare parts and equipment needed in Vietnam by American forces!

He revealed in January of 1969: *"The same machinery I couldn't get, the same equipment that would have saved the lives of those marines was declared 'non-strategic' and shipped to the very countries that supplied the rifles and bullets that are killing our men!*

"I remember visiting the Sixty -Seventh Evacuation Hospital in Qui Nhon.

"Walking through the intensive-care ward, I saw dozens of soldiers who had been maimed and mutilated.

"They had lost arms or legs, they were covered with plastic and swathed in bandages stained deep red by their own blood.

"Most were in agonizing pain or under 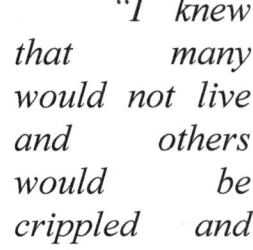 *heavy sedation.*

"I knew that many would not live and others would be crippled and disfigured for life.

"Seeing this bitter fruit of our government's madness I wondered how our politicians would try to explain to these men about sending 'non-strategic' items to an enemy that has pledged to destroy us."

The *"politicians"* never bothered!

Nor did any of them intend to!

A new era in treason was begun within weeks after Senator Barry Goldwater lost his Presidential bid in 1964.

The radicalized Johnson Administration officially sanctioned a traitorous trip to wheel and deal for expanded business behind the Iron Curtain.

Allen and Scott reported on December 16, 1964: *"More than 200 U.S. businessmen made the journey to Moscow . . . a few U.S. firms with a big assist from the State and Commerce Department [sent] representatives for extended stays of one to three months. "*

The Honorable Ezra Taft Benson correctly charged in 1968: *"In the waiting rooms of the Kremlin American businessmen dream of personal gains and profits while thousands of American*  *boys in Vietnam are slain by Communist bullets made in the USSR. "*

Peter Stark was a brave young Green Beret who lost both legs in combat against Communist Occupied North Vietnam.

He charged: *"America's leaders have assured the Soviet Union and its satellite nations who supply 80 percent of all the North Vietnamese war material that we will not interfere in their shipment of war goods to the North Vietnamese enemy.*

"At the same time we have continued our policy of sending strategic materials to the Soviet enemy.

"For example, in 1966, the United States sent the Soviet Union the entire

technical specification that they needed to build a glycerol plant.

"Specifically, in Vietnam, glycerol is used as a detonator in booby traps. Over 50 percent of all American casualties suffered in Vietnam have come from booby traps."

Yes, while the war in Vietnam raged the United States merrily aided, fed, traded with, loaned money to and armed America's avowed Communist enemies throughout the world.

 Treasonous American officials from the President on down knew all along that Communist Occupied Russia and her satellite clones were helping Ho chi Minh!

According to Professor David Nelson Rowe: *"The Russians supplied heavy weapons including surface-to-air missiles, tanks and artillery, as well as oil, all shipped into North Vietnam by ocean transport."*

Communist *People's World* of November 5, 1966, reported: *"The dense AA gun and the sophisticated radar network are all supplied by the USSR."*

34

America's leaders also knew that four man teams of Russian Spetsnaz commandoes spent time in Vietnam testing a new 7.62 mm sniper rifle by shooting U.S. soldiers.

"The USSR is heavily committed to helping North Vietnam in its aggressive designs against South Vietnam," charged Congressman Glenard P. Lipscomb on September 2, 1965. *"The Soviet Union has trained North*  *Vietnamese pilots to fly the MIG-21 Russian jet fighter.*

"Russian trawlers are located off Guam to provide early warnings of B-52 strikes on Viet Cong concentrations in South Viet Nam [captured Vietcong boasted how they  *always had a two hour advance notice of a B-52 bomber attack].*

"Does it make any sense to help equip and feed the Soviets who are helping the aggressors kill our soldiers in Vietnam?

"Tons of food and equipment were being sent by ship to North Vietnam," reported *Izvestia* on December 22, 1966. *"Some of the supplies included "tractors,*

cables and paper, medical equipment and canned goods and flour as part of the aid rendered by the Soviet people."

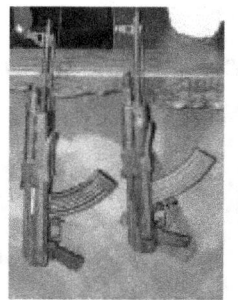

In addition Communist Occupied Russia supplied Hanoi with trucks, road building machinery, small ships, transport planes and jet fighters, amphibious vehicles, machine guns, mortars, grenade launchers, rockets and helicopters.

Poland, Czechoslovakia, Romania, and other Soviet slave-state clones also supplied the North Vietnamese enemy with war goods.

Their contributions included rifles, explosives and missile launchers all which were used to kill American military men.

Senator Clifford P. Hansen warned in 1968: *"American servicemen are dying this minute in Vietnam, killed by weapons which are the direct result of the various forms of trade that we have fostered and encouraged with Communist Satellite countries."*

Russia was supplied with the technical data necessary to build three huge fertilizer plants.

Meanwhile our Soviet *"friends"* were shipping over 150,000 tons of fertilizer to Communist Occupied North Vietnam.

The Vietnamese Reds in turn were slaughtering American boys!

Yet another outrageously criminal fertilizer plant deal was later consummated between the USSR and the Nixon Administration!

All this was taking place while Russian dictator Leonid Brezhnev openly acknowledged his active support of the North Vietnamese gangsters!

Brezhnev boasted in January of 1969: *"Hanoi would have been unable to keep up its heroic struggle for so many years without the active and effective assistance of the Soviet Union, Poland and other Socialist countries."*

According to the Department of Commerce there was a dramatic 44 percent jump in American trade with Communist Bloc dictatorships during the first half of 1966.

Why?

These are the same criminal regimes who were supplying North Vietnam with better than 85 percent of their war-making capability!

The Export-Import Bank guaranteed a $20 million loan to Communist Occupied Romania.

Why?

Because tyrannical slave master Nicolae Ceausescu wanted to buy an oil refinery!

Leftist Senator William Fulbright parroted the Kremlin propaganda line: *"Romania has demonstrated its interest in improving relations with the United States."*

Just the day before, on July 25, 1965, Red Romania publicly declared its support for the North Vietnamese and Chinese

Communists who were killing and maiming American military personnel on the battlefield.

Strom Thurmond said this on July 26, 1965: *"The Romanian Communist Congress meeting with representatives of Red China and Soviet Russia passed a resolution condemning the United States acts of open war in Vietnam."*

Johnson pushed hard to give Communist occupied Eastern European countries Most Favored Nation trade benefits.

He also demanded fewer restrictions on exporting strategic military-related items!

The President wanted more materials available for shipping to a variety of hate-America slave labor dictatorships!

LBJ made this treasonous statement in his October 7, 1966 speech to the National Conference of Editorial Writers: *"I have just today signed a determination that will allow the Export-Import Bank to guarantee commercial credits to four additional Eastern European countries -- Poland and Hungary, Bulgaria and Czechoslovakia.*

"We do not intend to let our differences on Vietnam or elsewhere prevent us from exploring all opportunities.

"Our differences" noted by the Commander-in-Chief of America's Armed Forces just happened to be an undeclared war with over 200,000 American casualties!

Each of the above mentioned Communist nations was vocally and materially aiding the North Vietnamese enemy!

Arch-enemy Communist Occupied Czechoslovakia broadcast: *"The entire [Communist] world has joined to provide Vietnam with all conceivable assistance."*

 Dictator Todor Zhivkov bragged in June of 1957 how *"the Bulgarian government has extended and will continue to extend material aid."*

Hungary's despotic Janos Kadar declared at the same time: *"We are fighting against U.S. aggression in Vietnam and will go on helping our Vietnamese brothers until their cause is crowned by ultimate victory."*

"After Congress had established a forbidden list of hundreds of items, nobody in America could ship to any Communist country sending supplies to the enemy," noted Senator Karl Mundt in his August 1967 speech to the National Convention of the American Legion, *"President Lyndon Johnson, on October 12,*  *1966, by Executive Order, in defiance of the expressed intentions and desires of Congress -- opened up for unlimited and unlicensed* shipment over 400 items of supplies to Russia and her satellites in Europe."

The list of crucial military supplies no longer  classed as *strategic* was absolutely incredible!

Cleared for export to enemy Communist regimes were such things as scrap metals, aluminum, grease, lubricating oil, diesel fuel, machine tools, tires and tubes, aircraft parts and navigation equipment, electric motors, synthetic rubber, steel tubing, copper cable, diethylene glycol (used to make explosives and liquid propellants for rockets), precision grinding machines, drilling machines, electrical machinery, ground and shipboard radar and diesel engines.

Communist Occupied Poland and Romania had previously been allowed special trade benefits by the Johnson Administration.

Red Czechoslovakia, Hungary, Albania, Yugoslavia, Bulgaria and the Russians were all now to be recipients of trade activities instigated by treasonous American government officials.

The Commerce Department's October 12, 1966, 68-page Commodity List classed strategic items as *"peaceful goods which may be freely exported [to enemy Red dictatorships] without any risks to the United States' national interest."*

Here are more of the goodies made

non-strategic with the stroke of the pen: rifle cleaning compounds, gasoline, petroleum drilling and production equipment, turbines, rocket and jet engines, generators, computers, ball bearings, rubber processing machines, railway equipment (trains, etc.), pipeline compressors, radiation detection instruments and radio beacon transmitters.

Soviet missiles directed by American computers downed many American fighter planes and helicopters in Vietnam.

Such a thing during World War II would have been called treason in no uncertain terms!

What exactly should we call it today?

Two weeks later our new and favored trade partners were in the news again.

According to the *New York Times* of October 27, 1966: *"The Soviet Union and its allies agreed at the conference of their leaders in Moscow last week to grant North Vietnam assistance in material and money amounting to about one billion dollars. Poland's contribution will be thirty million dollars."*

The *Chicago Tribune* of December 26, 1966 had to this to say about America's Polish pal: *"Weapons of the Polish armed forces are being shipped from Stettin harbor in Poland in ever increasing quantities to North Vietnam.*

"While on one side of the Stettin harbor American wheat is being unloaded from freighters, on the other side of the same harbor weapons are loaded that are being used to kill American soldiers.

"The Poles receive the wheat from the U.S. on credit, and they in turn ship their weapons to North Vietnam on credit."

Ambassador Averill Harriman was a long-term leftist and apologist for the Communists.

He was America's first representative at the Paris-based Vietnam surrender negotiations in 1966.

44

While there Harriman made his views clear regarding aid and trade with Communist countries.

He made the absurd comment on national television that all foes of Red trade in his opinion were *"bigoted, pig-headed people who don't know what's going on in the world."*

Former POW and Medal of Honor recipient Rear Admiral James Stockdale noted in his 1984 book, *In Love and War*: *"It was Averill Harriman who insisted on keeping the torture evidence under wraps in the interest*  *of furthering his 'delicate' negotiations on the prisoner's behalf, all of which came to nothing."*

Congressman Lipscomb revealed in 1968 that the Johnson Administration had *"clamped a tight lid on information showing just how much and what type of aid is being sent to Hanoi by the Communist bloc."*

Why the big secret?

Because it was blatant treason!

Because by mid 1967 Communist Occupied Russia had contributed $2 billion worth of war materials to North Vietnam.

Other Red bloc satellites are known to have sent at least $1 billion more in military aid.

There were nearly 10,000 Soviet-supplied anti-aircraft guns installed in North Vietnam.

More than 30 Soviet-supplied SAM batteries each capable of firing six surface-to-air missiles were operational.

Not only did the Russians provide the weapons they also trained the North Vietnamese military to more efficiently kill Americans.

The *Reporter* of January 1967 disclosed: *"The Soviet experts train their students in or near Hanoi and then go with them to the actual battle stations to see how they do under fire.*

"More coaching follows on the spot so it is almost inevitable that the Soviet officers actually man the radar screens and the missile launching devices."

General John P. McConnell, USAF Chief of Staff charged in June of 1967 that North Vietnam's Russian-supplied air defense system was *"the greatest concentration of anti-aircraft weapons that has ever been known in the history of defense of any town or in any area of the world."*

Congressman Lipscomb had this to say in 1967: *"Practically every American plane shot down over North Vietnam has fallen victim to Soviet-made and Soviet-supplied surface-to-air missiles or anti -aircraft batteries. American planes have been tracked by Soviet [American] radar.*

"American ground forces have been subjected to substantial casualties caused by Soviet and East European [American] equipment; and the Vietcong and North Vietnamese have been supplied in the South by trucks made in these countries [in American factories]."

Ships from Communist Occupied Russia and Red Bloc slave labor tyrannies off-loading in Haiphong Harbor were immune from being bombed or even fired upon!

How could this be?

According to the *Associated Press Wire Service of* September 13, 1967: *"The Pentagon has given North Vietnam official word that port facilities of Haiphong are safe from attack.*

"Their safety was guaranteed by President Johnson!"

Communist ships came at the rate of one every other day.

Many of the Soviet ships bringing war supplies to North Vietnam were built jn the United States!

Among them were the Tashkent, Bakuriani, Sevastopol, Voybou, Kubyshev, Ala-Tau, Suchan and the Kura.

Five of these vessels were World War II Liberty ships!

They'd been loaned to Communist Occupied Russia under the *Lend Lease* program.

The Soviets never bothered to return any of them!

On September 23, 1967, an official Soviet communiqué promised even more *"aircraft, anti-aircraft guns, ground-to-air missiles, artillery pieces, small arms, ammunition, and also equipment, vehicles, products and other goods."*

Here we have American military men being slaughtered in Vietnam by enemy soldiers who are armed, fed, and trained by Communist Occupied Russia.

This slave labor dictatorship was at the time being armed by the United States; obtaining loans from the United States; being fed by the United States; and being given preferential trade treatment by the United States!

Without monumental support from the Communist Bloc nations North Vietnam's ability to fight a war would have collapsed!

Without monumental American aid trade and loans Russia and her Red-slave satellites' ability to assist North Vietnam would have collapsed!

The United States was sending untold thousands of tons of strategic military goods to each and every one of these homicidal regimes!

In 1967 America's Polish *"friends"* were unable to even pay the interest on outstanding loans of $17 million.

President Lyndon Baines Johnson spoke before the National Conference of Editorial Writers on October 7, 1966. He unabashedly declared that he wanted to ease *"the burden of Polish debts to the United States."*

In other words, he wanted to let the Red slave labor dictatorship off the hook!

Treason?

Yes!

On April 12, 1967, the State Department announced it had worked out a deal to *forgive* the massive debts of the criminal despots who were running the Polish dictatorship.

Former Representative Paul Findley charged in the *Congressional Record* of April 13, 1967: *"By relieving Poland of the need to pay the $17 million debt in dollars, our Government has thus enabled Poland to aid the enemy at a level it otherwise could not afford."*

For example on April 12, 1967, Polish merchant ships were seen unloading military supplies in North Vietnam's Haiphong Harbor!

At the same time, the Communist government of Poland announced a mammoth demonstration to show support of the Communist cause in Vietnam.

Another traitorous activity was exposed by Congressman Edward J. Derwinski in a letter dated August 14, 1967: *"U.S. Army engineers are working on a highway over*

which supplies could move from Russia to North Vietnam.

"More specifically, the highway in question is being constructed under the foreign aid program across Afghanistan and thus would be a link between Russia and North Vietnam."

The highway was designed by Americans!

Its construction supervised by Americans!

It was paid for using American dollars!

Shockingly this highway was actually built while Americans were fighting and dying in the dictatorship the highway was going to; in a war being managed and financed by the dictatorship the highway was coming from!

And in December, 1979, Soviet troops invading Afghanistan were transported on this very same highway in military vehicles built in the American designed and supplied and financed Kama River truck factory.

Dangerous security risk Nicholas deB Katzenbach was Johnson's Attorney General.

He spoke to the National Association of  Manufacturers on December 9, 1967. In reference to trade with Communist dictatorships who were arming North Vietnam Katzenbach said such trade was *"good business, good policy, and good sense."*

The Communist organized and led street revolutionaries were closer to the truth than they realized with their slogan: *"Hey, hey, LBJ! -- How many boys did you kill today?"*

Exports of strategic goods to enemy Communist dictatorships surpassed $100 million during the first six months of 1968.

Close to $20 million worth was food!

The rest were highly sophisticated goods of a technical, military and military related nature.

The kinds of military items sent to the Reds were protected by a *"Top Secret"* classification!

Why?

Isn't the answer obvious?

In 1968, America's extensive food commodity exports alone to Communist Occupied Russia averaged an incredible $4 million per week.

A number of Congressmen including Karl E. Mundt, H. R. Gross and James B. Utt were against Johnson's treasonous giveaways to the Communists.

Senator Peter H. Dominick offered this in 1968: *"Administration pressures on Congress for trade expansion with the Communist-controlled countries of Eastern Europe, including the Soviet Union, multiply day by day at the very time when our men in*  *Vietnam are being killed by Soviet weapons.*

"Johnson and Nixon both criminally undermined anti-Communist allies of the United States while at the same time glorifying Red dictatorships."

For example friendly and free as well as anti-Communist Rhodesia volunteered to send troops to assist the United States in Vietnam.

The offer was rejected by leftist American policy makers!

Why?

All trade with America's Rhodesian ally was barred by Johnson's *Executive Order* dated July 29, 1968.

Why?

On March 17, 1970 Nixon further betrayed Rhodesia by shutting down the American Consulate!

Why?

All during this time, LBJ and Nixon hypocritically expanded trade with Communist Occupied Russia and other Red enemies.

Treason?

Absolutely!

Each was openly supplying Communist Occupied North Vietnam.

Presidential candidate Richard M. Nixon said in a national radio speech on October 24, 1968: *"As all Americans bitterly know the Soviets have been and still are the arsenal and the trainers of the North*

Vietnamese and have escalated this jungle battle into a major war."

In November of 1971, Nixon the President sent his Commerce Secretary Maurice Stans to Moscow to work out the details of a $2 billion strategic trade deal with the Russian dictatorship.

According to Stans: *"We have eliminated some 1800 items from the restrictions against sale to the Soviet Union and that process is still continuing."*

These 1800 items could now be sold to the USSR and other enemy countries in the Communist Bloc.

Included were even more priceless electronic equipment, tooling and machinery that the Russian Bear desperately needed for the production of war goods!

While campaigning for the Presidency James Earl Carter expressed no sympathy for the armless, legless, blind or otherwise mutilated heroes who made it back from Vietnam and

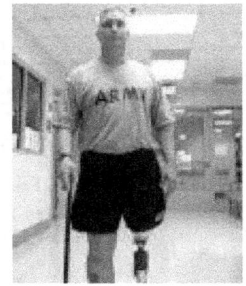

ended up in VA hospitals.

Nor did this pretentious *"born again Christian"* while campaigning for the Presidency say anything about the POWs left behind in Southeast Asia after Henry Kissinger had shut down the war!

Instead he shamelessly declared: *"During my first week in office, I would issue pardons to all Vietnam defectors."*

Yes, the traitors and cowards who ran and left their fellow Americans to fight, to die, to suffer capture by the bestial Communist enemy were rewarded by this President!

Carter couldn't wait but a day.

His first official act as President was to announce a *"full, complete and unconditional pardon"* on January 21, 1977 for all Vietnam draft-dodgers.

He even went so far as to upgrade the discharges of military men who hadn't served honorably in Vietnam.

Jane Fonda's most despicable deeds took place during the summer of 1972.

This traitor visited Communist Occupied North Vietnam and made Tokyo Rose type broadcasts over Radio Hanoi.

USAF Colonel George E. Day charged: *"When I was a prisoner of war in North Vietnam, Tom Hayden and Jane Fonda went on Radio Hanoi and called for American soldiers to throw down their weapons and stop fighting.*

"Clearly Tom Hayden and Jane Fonda committed acts of treason against the United States during a time of war."

Hanoi Jane was photographed while proudly sitting sat at the controls of a North Vietnamese anti-aircraft gun.

She peered through the sights while posing for propaganda pictures and expressed her *"solidarity"* with the Communist soldiers manning the weapon.

The Benedict Arnold of Beverly Hills forced herself on American POWs and tried to get them to make statements in support of the Communist-led *"peace"* movement.

POWs who refused to talk to Hanoi Jane were tortured and severely beaten!

So were those who did listen but were not persuaded by her rhetorical garbage!

Navy Lieutenant Commander David Hoffman revealed how the North Vietnamese used torture in order to force him to meet with Fonda.

Accompanying Hanoi Jane was former Attorney General Ramsey Clark!

Hoffman recalled: *"I had a broken arm.*

"It was in a cast.

"I was hung by that broken arm several times and allowed to drop at the end of a rope from a table which was kicked out from under me."

The *Trenton Times* told the story of *"a POW who had agreed to meet with some other Americans in the 'peace' movement.*

"The 'peace' people commanded the POW to confess to war crimes.

"When he repeatedly and adamantly refused he heard a 'peace' person suggest to his captors that 'this young man needs to be straightened out in his thinking.'

"He was hung by his wrists until an arm pulled from its shoulder socket.

"Other prisoners suffering similar abuse also were made to suffer Jane Fonda's voice: The North Vietnamese piped into the cells recordings in which she urged prisoners to actively oppose U.S. policy, and told the world how well the prisoners were being treated."

Hanoi Jane returned from North Vietnam after two full weeks of socializing with her murderous hosts.

This traitor and her husband Tom Hayden had deliberately betrayed America's fighting men and their country to the Communist enemy!

Hayden blatantly lied in June of 1971 when he claimed that American POWs weren't tortured. He claimed: *"They were the best treated prisoners in any war in history."*

Hanoi Jane blatantly lied when she agreed!

Returning POWs contested this with firsthand experiences of brutality, torture, and murder.

Hayden spoke for himself and Hanoi Jane when he called the POWs *"liars, hypocrites and pawns."*

James Ray of Conroe, Texas, declared: *"I would personally challenge that young lady to look at the scars still visible on my arms from the tortures and tell me to my face that I'm a liar and a hypocrite."*

Chief Warrant Officer Roy E. Zeigler II spent five years in a North Vietnamese prison.

He responded: *"Liars, hypocrites and pawns are we?*

"Men died at the hands of their captors and you have the audacity to say we were the best treated prisoners in any war in history."

Former Congressman Robert H. Steele nominated Oscar-winning Hanoi Jane for a special award: *"The rottenest, most miserable performance by any one individual American in the history of our country.*

"Where does she get her colossal gall?

"I wonder if she would dare to make her charges to the faces of those men who were beaten with rifle butts in the jungle or to the captured airman who was tied down with wire while ants swarmed over his body until he thought he would be eaten alive?"

Congressman Robert J. Huber was outraged at the behavior of Fonda.

He stated in December of 1985: *"Examined from the evidentiary focus of a grand jury, the testimony of my colleagues establishes sufficient factual allegations to support indictments against Jane Fonda on the ground of conspiracy and under the Sedition Act (18 U.S.C. 2387)."*

"She and others like her were traitors," charged Lieutenant Colonel James Thompson who was for almost nine nightmarish years a POW *"and I see no reason why she shouldn't be hung for it!"*

But such indictments were never to come!

Hanoi Jane got off scot-free!

Why?

She was never even brought to trial.

Why?

In fact, she wasn't even charged with anything!

Why?

How could she or anyone else do so much harm to her country and still get away with it?

Her rewards?

Over and above a Hollywood Oscar in a personal affront to every American veteran Hanoi Jane Fonda was invited to attend a White House  reception on November 17, 1977.

Why?

President *(Trust Me)* Carter honored her in this manner a little more than five years after she had pulled her traitorous shenanigans in Hanoi during 1972!

Newsweek was not unfriendly to Fonda. It called her *"a modern day LaPasionaria if not quite yet a Mother Bloor."*

This should give everyone a clue about Fonda's politics should there be any question.

LaPasionaria was a fanatical Red leader during the Communist insurrection in Spain which was misleadingly called the Spanish Civil War.

Ella Reeva *"Mother"* Bloor was a revered Communist during the 1930s in the United States.

She was the mother of Harold Ware who was a most important Kremlin espionage agent.

Ware had been sent to America by Stalin to direct the initial penetration of the government through the Department of Agriculture.

Thomas Emmett Hayden is one of the few leftist revolutionaries in the United States whose record of treasonous acts and traitorous deeds exceeds those of his radicalized wife.

Hayden was a founder of the subversive Students for a Democratic Society.

This was the parent organization of the Weather Underground which was a Communist anti-American terrorist group.

Hayden had been to Hanoi with Communist Party leader Herbert Aptheker and others long before Jane Fonda had even heard of the place.

Evidently well-connected this radical moved about freely throughout the Red Bloc nations while Ho Chi Minh's Communists were slaughtering American boys in Vietnam.

Charged J. Edgar Hoover in June of

1968: *"The aim of the SDS attack is to smash first our educational structure, then our economic system, then, finally our government itself."*

One of Hayden's criminal cohorts was Bernadine Dohrn who was an SDS official.

She called herself a *"revolutionary Communist."*

Hayden was a highly trained professional agitator who led the Communist organized riots at Columbia University in April and May of 1968.

He also directed the violent Red demonstrations at the 1968 Democratic National Convention in Chicago.

This notorious subversive was convicted under the anti-riot provisions of the *Civil Rights Act.*

Hayden was sentenced to five years in prison and given a $5,000 fine.

His conviction was conveniently reversed by a leftist federal judge.

Tom Hayden would have been hanged for treason during World War II for doing the things he did while the Vietnam War raged.

Both he and Fonda were unquestionably responsible for the further suffering and torture of American POWs.

USAF Colonel George E. Day was a POW during the Vietnam War.

He wrote in November of 1987: *"He's a traitor to this great nation and deserves to be treated as one."*

Instead the radical bomb throwing leader of the violent SDS was warmly welcomed to the White House oval office by President Carter in February of 1978!

Hayden tells in June of 1987 how Carter said *"he was proud to meet me and started talking about the contributions that I had made to the country."*

Incredible?

Yes, but true nonetheless!

Red rabble-rouser Jerry Rubin set up a foundation to shelter his earnings. It was given a tax exempt status by the Nixon Administration.

Why?

Massachusetts Senator John Forbes Kerry was a leading activist with the ultra-radical Vietnam Veterans Against the War.

Kerry led Pro-Vietcong demonstrations that welcomed *"revolutionary Communists."*

According to the *Boston Herald Traveler* of December 12, 1971, the demonstrations were *"characterized by an abundance of Vietcong flags, clenched fists raised [a symbolic Communist gesture] and placards plainly bearing legends in support of China, Cuba, the USSR, North Korea and the Hanoi government."*

When asked about Communist participation in his shameless anti-American efforts Kerry said it was *"not relevant."*

The media did nothing to challenge this lie!

Nguyen khac Vien was a North Vietnamese propagandist. He said this: *"Our country has no capability to defeat you on the battlefield.*

"But war is not decided by weapons so much as national will.

"We will win this war on the streets of New York."

And so they did!

Kerry and company saw to it that this was exactly what happened!

This radical leftist appeared on *Meet the Press* and insultingly called American leaders *"war criminals."*

He knew better!

John Forbes Kerry was a liar!

Kerry falsely accused American fighting men of committing *"all kinds of atrocities"* in Vietnam.

He knew better!

John Forbes Kerry was a liar!

John Forbes Kerry a traitor?

Of course he was!

70

In 1984, this same anti-American misfit cleaned up his act!

And the people of Massachusetts bought it hook, line and sinker!

Apparently the voters either had a short memory span or they were abjectly ignorant.

Kerry became their junior United States Senator!

True to form his subsequent traitorous support of the Red Sandinistas in Communist Occupied Nicaragua earned him the nickname *"The Senator from Managua."*

According to Senator Barry Goldwater in February of 1987 Kerry had violated the *Logan Act* by privately negotiating with the Communists.

Yet he was never punished!

Why?

Because the rewards for being an anti-American pro-Communist Vietcong supporter were great! In the case of a traitor the likes of

John Forbes Kerry it was to eventually become our Secretary of State.

Many other traitors who had treasonously aided and abetted the Communist enemy were well taken care of by the moles throughout the very government they so vocally despised.

Just a few years before, these radicals were in the streets leading treasonous demonstrations in support of the country's battlefield enemy!

Shortly thereafter these unkempt recreants were then cleaned up and were avidly recruited for important positions in the Carter Administration.

President James Earl Carter's most influential advisor and his *"closest friend in the world"* was British born psychiatrist Peter G. Bourne.

This radical was a promoter of anti-American causes from the time of his arrival in the United States, in 1957.

Ironically Bourne was a drug user himself.

He became Director of the Office of Drug Abuse Policy and Special Advisor to the President for Health Issues.

He took a leading part in Tom Hayden's Communist-run demonstrations during the 1968 Democratic National Convention in Chicago.

Carter's *"closest friend in the world"* was also a close pal of leftist John Kerry.

He co-founded the violence-prone, pro-Vietcong Vietnam Veteran's Against the War.

This Communist group undertook paramilitary operations and engaged in rioting during the Republican National Convention in Miami.

Mary King was Bourne's militant leftist wife.

This radical was Carter's top female appointee.

She'd been the Communications Coordinator for Marxist Stokely Carmichael's Student Non-Violent Coordinating Committee.

This leftist became Deputy Director of ACTION under Samuel Winfred Brown.

Brown was a Harvard Divinity School dropout and an anti-American pro-Vietcong activist.

This leftist openly declared in 1969 that he was all for a Communist victory in Vietnam.

He'd worked hard for the defeat of his own nation!

Brown's efforts in behalf of the enemy had the United States been in a declared war would have resulted in his execution for treason!

Yet both the Constitutional definition of treason as well as the Federal statutes mentions nothing about only in cases of a declared war.

Sam Brown was well rewarded for his enthusiastic support of Ho Chi Minh and the Vietnamese Reds.

He became Carter's $52,000-a-year head of ACTION an umbrella agency which ran the Peace Corps and VISTA.

From here Brown proceeded to give outrageous grants to his various pro-Red cronies!

According to Margery A. Tabankin's resume she *"was also active in the anti-war movement, and visited American prisoners of war and government officials in North Vietnam."*

Tabankin took part in interrogations of American POWs who were imprisoned and tortured by the North Vietnamese Communists!

Tabankin's treasonous role in working on behalf of the North Vietnamese enemy should have warranted her execution for treason!

It didn't!

Why?

Patrick Buchanan wrote: *"Marge junketed to Hanoi at the height of the war, while American POWs were down the street at the Hanoi Hilton being tortured in Uncle Ho's prison.*

"Today, this Axis Sally of the Vietnam War takes home a higher federal salary than almost all of the young American pilots accused of war crimes."

At the very least it should have prohibited her from ever holding a government job!

Yet this out and out traitor was also nicely rewarded for her anti-American pro-Viet Cong efforts.

Tabankin was one of radical Sam Brown's close activist pals.

As a result of this friendship she was well rewarded by being placed in charge of ACTION education programs.

Quite a number of other anti-American, pro-Hanoi activists could be found implanted throughout the Carter Administration.

Such radicals include Arabella Martinez who became Assistant Secretary for Human Development in HEW.

Another was James A. Joseph who became Under Secretary of the Interior.

While working for the Irwin-Miller-Sweeney Foundation Joseph had channeled finances to Communist revolutionaries during the 1960s.

Dangerous leftist Alex P. Mecure became Assistant Secretary of Agriculture for Rural Development.

Mecure was once on the board of directors of the radical Center for Community Change.

This subversive group gave birth to the anti-CIA *Counter-Spy* which was directly responsible for the exposure and assassination by Communist terrorists of CIA agent Richard Welch in Greece.

Mecure's group also spun off the tax exempt *Youth Liberation Project* once headed by Margery Tabankin. They trained young people in murder techniques and in the latest arson methods.

Tax Exempt?

Why?

James M. Fallows was a self-proclaimed coward and Harvard radical. He was editor of the leftist *Washington Monthly*.

He bragged in November of 1977 about how he'd faked his draft-board physical *"because I was desperately afraid of being killed."*

His leftist counselors had illegally advised him and his anti-war pals that *"disruptive behavior at the examination . . . obstructed the smooth operation of the criminal war machine."*

Fallows proudly told how many in his group demonstrated while wearing *"red arm bands and stop-the-war buttons . . . most chanted the familiar words 'Ho, Ho, Ho Chi Minh/NLF Is Gonna Win!'"*

These radicals did everything possible to disrupt the examinations including throwing warm urine into the faces of orderlies!

Unbelievable as it may sound, this unprosecuted Vietnam draft-dodger was eventually rewarded with an influential, high-paying job as President Carter's chief speechwriter!

Hendrick Hertzberg was a contributing editor of *Win*.

This was a publication of the socialist War Resisters League which worked closely with the Soviet World Peace Council in support of Red terror groups worldwide.

Hertzberg's Communist bias was clearly revealed in October of 1980 when he said : *"It would be undeniably 'better' for the United States alone to be destroyed than for the Soviet Union, Europe and much of the rest of the world to be destroyed as well."*

In May 1976 while actively supporting the Communist enemy in Vietnam he said: *"I welcome their victory."*

Despite the horrible atrocities up to and accompanying the Communist occupation of South Vietnam Hertzberg said the Red takeover *"was a moral victory"* and *"a victory for something honorable in the human spirit."*

Incredibly this anti-American misfit was presented with a salary gift of $32,500 a year to assist Fallows in writing speeches for President James Earl Carter!

Hertzberg's asinine *"moral victory"* ignored the words of Robert E. Lee who revealed: *"In 1946, after Ho chi Minh established his troops in Hanoi, there were two indigenous Vietnamese sects in the area which, because they were also fervently anti-Communist, represented a future potential threat to Ho's plans.*

"So he decided to have them exterminated.

"Since routine murder would have fallen short of the desired impact on others, he resorted instead to burying members of the two sects alive in fields, so that only their heads were above the ground, then having harrows driven back and forth across the fields, as one report later described it, to 'scratch and tear and chop those living heads like so many small tree stumps as the harrows went over them."

Tom Dooley was an American missionary who witnessed extensive Communist brutality.

In one instance North Vietnamese soldiers visited a school.

The teacher and seven students were dragged outside and bound.

In Dooley's words: *"The Viet Minh accused these children of treason.*

"As a punishment they were to be deprived of their hearing.

"Two Viet Minh guards went to each child and rammed a wooden chopstick into each ear.

"The stick split the ear canal wide and tore the ear drum.

"The shrieking of the children was heard all over the village.

"Since their hands were tied behind them, they could not pull the wood out of their ears.

"They shook their heads and squirmed about, trying to make the sticks fall out.

"Finally they were able to dislodge

them by scraping their heads against the ground.

"As for the teacher -- one soldier held his head while another grasped the victim's tongue with a crude pair of pliers and pulled it far out.

"A third guard cut off the top of the teacher's tongue with his bayonet.

"Blood spurted into the man's mouth and gushed from his nostrils.

"When the soldiers let him loose he fell to the ground vomiting blood."

Priests are commonly selected for special treatment by the Communists.

Many of the most hideous atrocities are reserved for *"treason"* which is simply the act of teaching about Jesus and God.

Dr. Dooley further reported: *"There was an old man lying on straw on the floor.*

"His head was matted with pus and there were eight large pus-filled swellings around his temple and fore-head.

"Eight nails had been driven into his head, three across the fore-head, two in the back of the skull and three across the dome.

"When the unbelievable act was completed, the priest walked from his church

to a neighboring hut, where a family jerked the nails from his head."

Accounts of Communist barbarianism, brutality, inhumanity and wanton slaughter are not isolated by any stretch of the imagination!

Such demonic activity is the rule rather than the exception in Communist occupied areas of the world.

In unconscionable acts of immorality American leaders turn their heads and ignore the truth.

They pretend these atheistic tyrants are worthy friends.

America builds them factories!

America feeds their slaves!

America arms their military!

America lends them untold millions of dollars!

As the heroic American patriot Robert Welch rightly said: *"May God forgive us."*

The Communists operate identically in every country they subjugate!

Vietnam was no different than Korea!

When the Communist North Koreans invaded South Korea they simply annihilated their opposition.

Robert Leckie reported: *"At Sachon the North Koreans burned the jail and 280 South Korean police, government officials and landowners who were inside it!*

At Anui, at Mokpo, at Kongju, and at Hamyang and Chonju, United Nations soldiers uncovered trenches stuffed with the bodies of hundreds of executed civilians, many of them women and children!

"Near Taejon airstrip 500 ROK soldiers lay with their hands bound behind their backs and bullet holes in their brains!"

The USS Pueblo was captured by Communist Occupied North Korea on January 23, 1968.

Commander Lloyd Bucher tells of an incident he witnessed while a prisoner of the bestial Reds: *"A South Korean was strapped to the wall . . . he was a South Korean spy.*

"He was alive, but had been through a terrible ordeal.

"He had a compound fracture of the upper right arm.

"The bone was sticking out.

"He was stripped to the waist.

"He had completely bitten through his lower lip, and his lower lip was hanging down from the side of his mouth.

"His right eye had been put out.

"His head was hanging down.

"There was a lot of black matter which had run out of his eye and down his cheek."

Dangerous revolutionary John Froines was one of the notorious Chicago Seven.

He was a rabid riot team pal of Communist Abbe Hoffman, Jerry Rubin and Rennie Davis (below).

They and Tom Hayden planned the violent disruptions at the 1968 Democratic National Convention.

Froines boldly boasted to a mob of unwashed anti-American-pro-Hanoi fanatics in the nation's capitol that he'd come to Washington to close down the government!

This pro-Communist Vietcong supporter also ended up with a soft job in the Carter Administration.

He was placed in charge of the Office of Toxic Substances at OSHA.

Many horrible deeds were committed by the Communist forces during their forcible takeover of South Vietnam.

These are but a few of the things that went on but were blatantly ignored by those many misguided individuals who traitorously supported the takeover of South Vietnam by the North Vietnamese savages.

Syndicated columnist Paul Scott reported on the fall of Saigon in the Spring of 1975: *"The most vicious bloodbath in modern history is now going on in South Vietnam.*

"The total number of persons killed or executed outright since the Communists started their takeover has soared to more than 250,000.
"In one instance, more than 400 helpless orphans and at least five nuns were put to death at one particular orphanage in DaNang and at an orphanage in China Beach.

"The region appears to be one of the main execution sites."

Aerial photographs taken of the China Beach area in early April showed more than 30,000 bodies of South Vietnamese people who had been executed by the Communists!

Clothes Taken From Headless Bodies in Mass Graves

"I well remember a little twelve-year old girl the Communists had dragged off a bus" offered Sergeant Alan L. Davidson in 1968. *"They had pulled her around to the side where all the passengers could look on in*

horror as one V.C. held her arm and another chopped it off with a machete.

"I remember wondering what the will to resist would be like in California if in but one year more than two thousand Mayors and City Councilmen were shot, beheaded or eviscerated in the main street of their communities and left with their blood to pool in the gutter.

"Precisely that happened in Vietnam.

"The Vietcong has systematically butchered some fifteen thousand local officials.

"The Communists have no regard for that life if its elimination will further the aims of the International Conspiracy in the slightest way."

John Dryden was a Green Beret in Vietnam.

He told of the horror he witnessed upon returning to a village after the Communists had come and gone: *"When I arrived at the outpost, it was impossible not to see my friends.*

"Their bodies were on one side of the highway, laid out as if for inspection, their heads on the other side.

"It was all militarily neat and orderly.

"Their wives and children, as befitting mere civilians, were not in ranks.

"They lay where they had been shot or bayoneted haphazardly.

"Every single living thing in that community was dead -- water buffalo, pigs, and dogs!"

West Point graduate Lieutenant Colonel Paul G. Erickson told this horror story: *"Before I left Saigon, I visited a government photo lab.*

"There they had more than 600,000 photographs of Communist atrocities against the Vietnamese people.

"I saw pictures of the charred bodies at Dak Son, where the Vietcong had turned flame throwers on several hundred defenseless men, women, and children!

"Many were of mutilated priests and nuns and hamlet chiefs since the village leaders were always a major target of the Communists.

"There were thousands of photographs of men who had been disemboweled, their eyeballs popped out and their throats cut in front of the entire populace!

"Nuns had been raped repeatedly by the Communists and then Christian villagers were forced at gunpoint to participate before the Sisters were murdered!"

Identified Soviet spy Henry *"Bor"* Kissinger as Nixon's subversive Secretary of State assured Americans that there'd be no bloodbath in South Vietnam!

So did Tom Wicker of the New York Times and numerous other wild-eyed leftists!

The New York Times ran this headline: INDOCHINA WITHOUT AMERICANS FOR MOST A BETTER LIFE.

Mary McGrory had the unmitigated gall to declare: *"The new leaders of South Vietnam are far too busy to draw a bloodbath.*

"They are behaving more like missionaries than conquerors."

McGrory's ignorance regarding her beloved conquerors was appalling to say the very least.

After the ruthless enslavement of South Vietnam was completed the Soviet Union obtained 500,000 *"Siberian volunteers"* from Hanoi!

Doan van Toai was a former Vietcong who defected.

He told how the ages of these slave laborers ranged from 17 to 35 years.

A half-million hapless Vietnamese were shipped to horrifying Soviet concentration camps unmatched by any the world has ever known!

They were exported to Communist Occupied Russia as partial payment for the trucks, anti-aircraft guns, surface-to-air missiles and other war goods their Soviet benefactor so willingly supplied during the Vietnam conflict.

Inhuman arrangements of this type have been undertaken with every country the USSR has assisted militarily or otherwise in a Communist takeover!

John Hubbell gives one horrifying example of an atrocity committed by the North Vietnamese Reds.

This tragic episode transpired in a small hamlet near Da Nang: *"All were herded before the home of their chief.*

"While they and the chief's pregnant wife and four children were forced to look on, the chief's tongue was cut out.

"Then his genital organs were sliced off and sewn inside his bloody mouth.

"As he died, the V.C. went to work on his wife, slashing open her womb.

"Then the nine year old son: a bamboo lance was rammed through one ear and out the other.

"Two more of the chief's children were murdered the same way.

"The V.C. did not harm the five year old daughter -- not physically; they left her crying holding her dead mother's arm."

The North Vietnamese did a variety of ghastly things to their captives while consolidating their control of South Vietnam.

Blood extraction was a favorite!

Fidel Castro carried out an identical program in Communist Occupied Cuba called *"Operation Blood Plasma."*

Blood was extracted from Cuban prisoners and then sold to help finance his Communist dictatorship!

Dr. Russell Kirk explained what happened to many South Vietnamese captives: *"Officials, military officers and other opponents of the Communists were sent to hospitals but not for the pretended 're-education' that Radio Hanoi and Radio Saigon propagandized about.*

"*In those Saigon hospitals the captives 'give' blood thus atoning for their former ways.*

"*But they are bled excessively; in a few days they are bled to death deliberately.*"

Hanoi Jane Fonda was evidently quite enthralled over the deeds of her atheistic mass-exterminator friends!

She spoke kindly of them in a speech she made at Michigan State University on November 22, 1969!

She jubilantly told some youthful college listeners: *"I would think that if you understood what Communism was you would hope, you would pray on your knees that we would someday become Communist!"*

These are the murderous fiends so glorified by Jane Fonda. She enthusiastically called them *"the conscience of the world!"*

This traitor spoke of the ungodly Vietcong barbarians as being *"driven by the same spirit that drove Washington and Jefferson!"*

The *Logan Act* was designed to stop private citizens from interfering with a President's exclusive Constitutionally guaranteed right to conduct America's foreign policy!

Its purpose is to also stop members of other branches of government -- Senators, Representatives, and judges -- from improperly interfering in foreign affairs!

The law is clear as to what constitutes a violation and the allowable criminal penalties!

One case is that of Congressman Jim Wright and nine others who signed the infamous *"Dear Commandante"* letter in support of Madison Avenue Daniel Ortega

the Communist dictator of Nicaragua.

`   The treasonous letter apologized for President Ronald Reagan's support of the anti-communist Contras and advised the tyrant on how to handle the public relations battle so as to get around the Reagan policies.

Wright and his Congressional traitors offered Sandinista leader Daniel Ortega a deal: Don't do anything too overtly Marxist.

Democrats would see to it that the Reagan-backed freedom fighters would be denied funding.

Treason?

No question about it !

Other examples of radical leftists who defiantly broke the Logan Act and thereby committed treason include Jane Fonda, Tom Hayden, Cora Weiss, David Dellinger, Rennie Davis, former Attorney General Ramsey Clark and hundreds of other Communists and pro-Communists who made treasonous trips to Communist Occupied Vietnam.

These traitors were illegally involved in private negotiations with the Red leadership in Hanoi.

Treason?

Without question !

Theirs was a deliberate effort to wreck American foreign policy under the guise of ending the Vietnam War.

Treason?

Certainly !

Stopping the war to these radicals simply meant an end to all opposition to the Communists in the North!

It meant letting South Vietnam fall to the enemy!

These traitors were openly contemptuous of the law!

They traveled abroad at will to meet with the Communist North Vietnamese leaders.

Their sole intention was to alter U.S. policy to favor the goals of the Communists!

There's absolutely no question but that Fonda and others of her ilk should have been indicted and tried at the very least under the *Logan Act*!

And they certainly should have been prosecuted for treason!

Unfortunately, they were not!

Why?

The Communist Party, the National Lawyers Guild, the ACLU and other radical groups worked to have the *Logan Act* repealed.

They falsely claimed it was somehow a dire threat to free speech, free association and all the rest of the usual leftist scare phrases.

Judge for yourself!

The language isn't difficult to understand: *"Any citizen of the United States, wherever he may be, who, without authority of the United States, directly or indirectly commences or carries on any correspondence or intercourse with any foreign government of any officer or any agent thereof, with intent to influence the measures or conduct of any foreign government of any officer or agent thereof, in relation to any disputes or controversies with the United States, or to defeat the measures of the United States, shall be fined not more than $5,000 or imprisoned not more than three years, or both."*

American POWs were tortured in order to force them to meet with American traitors who continually visited Hanoi during the Vietnam War!

Those collaborators many of them known Communists helped their North Vietnamese comrades by checking POW *"confessions"* for accuracy!

Why were American citizens allowed to go to Hanoi in the first place?

This question has never been answered!

Why didn't the government prosecute the hundreds of traitors who made these unauthorized trips to cavort with the enemy?

Why were none of these pro-Communists tried for treason?

The truth is simply that the Communist and pro-Communist revolutionaries doing all the traveling were being aided and abetted and protected by their Communist and pro-Communist revolutionary counterparts entrenched in our government!

Sybil Stockdale was the wife of the highest ranking navy POW.

She was officially informed that the passports of these traitors *"weren't stamped in North Vietnam and so there was no legal evidence that they'd been there, even when they broadcast the details of these trips on the front page of the newspapers."*

Hogwash!

The Department of Justice refused to enforce the *Logan Act* during the Vietnam War.

For example Ramsey Clark arrived in Hanoi from Moscow on July 29, 1972 *"on a two week visit as a guest of the North Vietnamese Government."*

While there he was interviewed for a propaganda broadcast on the Communist *Voice of Vietnam*!

Upon his return to the U.S. Clark held a news conference and said he *"believed that as a private citizen he had the right to go to North Vietnam and do what he could to try to bring peace and gain release of prisoners."*

Despite Clark's open acts of treason and his flaunting of the law Nixon's Attorney General Richard G. Kleindienst's response was incredible: *"I don't anticipate any Logan Act cases right now.*

"No evidence of any wrong doing has been presented to the Department yet."

Huh?

Epilogue

The record covering crucial episodes of the McCarthy era has been massively and deliberately distorted from the very beginning!

Conveniently forgotten or deliberately overlooked are the 78 hearings held between 1951 and 1952 by Senator William E. Jenner's (R-Indiana) Senate Internal Security Subcommittee (SISS); the House Committee On Internal Security; the House Un-American Activities Committee (HUAC) under the chairmanship of both Martin Dies (D-Texas) and Francis Walters (D-Pa); the Federal Bureau of Investigation (FBI) under the guidance of J. Edgar Hoover; and other investigating committees and individuals.

Out of all of these investigations one man was selected:

> To be stopped!
> To be destroyed!
> To be made an example!

Why?

So that no one would ever again dare to initiate any investigations into the penetration of our government agencies by communist agents (spies) in the employ of the Soviet Union!

Yes!

An obscure Senator from Wisconsin was deliberately targeted for this purpose!

Joseph McCarthy's incredibly successful investigations panicked those on the political left.

Their reaction was shockingly quick!

Key data was been suppressed, denied and even widely falsified.

This took place in the media, all branches of government and many alleged scholars entrenched in the ivory towers of our institutions of higher learning!

Such misreporting and misrepresentation of the facts continues today.

Much of the misinformation we were (and still are today) so carefully spoon-fed about Senator Joseph McCarthy the man and his investigations was no more than an admixture of uncheckable blovations from deceased third parties and demonstratable falsehoods!

For example, how many innocent people were harmed by McCarthy's revelations?

The correct answer?

Not one!

No!

Not One!

McCarthy's most virulent critics have had more than a half century to produce the names of the hundreds of innocent people they claim were destroyed by the astounding revelations of the Senator from Wisconsin.

Yet those highly skilled propagandists in our media and government and institutions of higher learning have been unable to name even one innocent person they claim was destroyed after being falsely accused by McCarthy!

How many innocent people committed suicide as a result of McCarthy's exposure?

The correct answer?

Not one!

Not one suicide can be attributed to the investigations conducted by McCarthy!

No! Not one!

According to the obscene claims made the highly skilled propagandists in our media, government and scholars entranced in those ivory towers of our colleges and universities there were a rash of suicides with bodies falling constantly of the heads of pedestrians below on the streets of Manhattan!

Once again, McCarthy's most virulent critics have had more than 50 years to produce the names of the hundreds of innocent people they claim committed suicide because of the astounding revelations of the Senator from Wisconsin.

Yet those highly skilled propagandists in our media and government and institutions of higher learning have been unable to name even one innocent person they claim committed suicide after being falsely accused by McCarthy!

No!

Not one!

But there were two suicides on record during the McCarthy period!

Neither was the result of an innocent person who'd been ruined by McCarthy's revelations!

Both were subversives who'd been exposed by McCarthy!

Both were subversives who'd been positively indentified as Kremlin agents!

Lawrence Duggan had been operating in the State Department as a widely known Soviet spy!

He'd been called to testify before a Congressional investigating committee.

Duggan never made it!

He conveniently "fell" from a window high up in a Manhattan skyscraper!

Fell?

Probably not!

He was more than likely pushed from or tossed out of the window by an assassin in the employ of the Soviet Union!

Why?

To make certain he didn't fold under pressure and start naming other Kremlin moles.

Secondly there was the unexpected demise of Harry Dexter White.

This Soviet agent discovered that he was being investigated by J. Edgar Hoover of the FBI!

He died of a sudden heart attack!

Coincidence?

Not hardly!

Was White's death a suicide?

Yes or at least so claimed McCarthy's critics!

Again, not hardly!

Heart attacks can readily be induced with the proper use of certain medicines administered by a hired assassin in the employ of the Kremlin!

Why?

Simply to eliminate anyone who might panic and decide to turncoat and reveal the names of other spies secretly entrenched deeply in the bowels of every branch of our government.

To sum up, most fit into one of three categories:

Conscience lacking incurable liars!

Those with an axe to grind!

Individuals who simply do not know the facts!

If you liked this book in the *None Dare Call It Treason* series then you'll probably also enjoy reading the others!

Gift copies of this book can be ordered at

createspace.com/4215293

Available Titles

None Dare Call It Treason Book 1
The Internal Security Farce!
5.5" x 8.5" 103 pages $4.95
Order from createspace.com/4215951

None Dare Call It Treason Book 2
Never Ending Subversion
In Government!
5.5" x 8.5" 99 pages $4.95
Order from createspace.com/4216385

None Dare Call It Treason Book 3
America's Subversive State Department
Bloated With Security Risks
5.5" x 8.5" 98 pages $4.95
Order from createspace.com/4216626

None Dare Call It Treason Book 4
America's Illustrious State Department!
It's Machiavellian Misdeeds!
5.5" x 8.5" 106 pages $4.95
Order from createspace.com/4215018

None Dare Call It Treason Book 5
Our Presidents A Major Security Threat!
5.5" x 8.5" 73 pages $4.95
Order from createspace.com/4213501

None Dare Call It Treason Book 6
Presidential Words & Deeds
&Blatant Lies!
5.5" x 8.5" 128 pages $4.95
Order from createspace.com/4213920

None Dare Call It Treason Book 7
Subversives Close To Our Presidents
5.5" x 8.5" 104 pages $4.95
Order from createspace.com/4213931

None Dare Call It Treason Book 8
Henry Kissinger
The Shadowy Untouchable Kremlin Spy!
5.5" x 8.5" 74 pages $4.95
Order from createspace.com/4214986

None Dare Call It Treason Book 9
Inexcusably Arming America's Enemies!
5.5" x 8.5" 102 pages $4.95
Order from createspace.com/4216634

None Dare Call It Treason Book 10
Inexcusably Financing
America's Enemies!
5.5" x 8.5" 102 pages $4.95
Order from createspace.com/4216777

None Dare Call It Treason Book 11
Treasonous   Trade With & Aid To
Enemies Of Freedom!
5.5" x 8.5" 93 pages $4.95
Order from createspace.com/4216873

None Dare Call It Treason Book 12
Wholesale Treason During the War
In Vietnam!
5.5" x 8.5" 120 pages $4.95
Order from createspace.com/4215293

None Dare Call It Treason Book 13
Big Business
& Astounding Acts Of Treason!
5.5" x 8.5" 93 pages $4.95
Order from createspace.com/4215805

None Dare Call It Treason Book 14
Illegally Importing
Slave Made Goodies!
5.5" x 8.5" 91 pages $4.95
Order from createspace.com/4215894

None Dare Call It Treason Book 15
The House That Hiss Built
The Anti-American United Nations!
5.5" x 8.5" 117 pages $4.95
Order from createspace.com/4215323

None Dare Call It Treason Book 16
Security Risks in the House and Senate!
5.5" x 8.5" 62 pages $4.95
Order from createspace.com/4213508

None Dare Call It Treason Book 17
*The Supreme Court A Devastating
Threat To National Security!*
5.5" x 8.5" 90 pages $4.95
Order from createspace.com/4213699

Orders for Resale
40% Off Retail Price

Send Purchase Order to

christianamerica2@yahoo.com

MEET
THE AUTHOR

Robert W. Pelton has been writing for more than 45 years on political and historical subjects.

He has published more than 100 books including the sensational *Unwanted Dead or Alive – An Expose of The Worst Act of Treason in Our History – The Betrayal of American POWs Following World War 11, Korea and Vietnam.*

Mr. Pelton proudly claims a heritage going all the way back to well before the War for American Independence.

One of his ancestors, John Rogers, came to America on the Mayflower and was one of 41 signers of the *Mayflower Compact.*

Another, John Smith was one of the founders of Jamestown.

Peleg Pelton served as the fifer in the Continental Army at age 17 during the Battle of Saratoga (1777) and again in Yorktown (1781).

Captain Peter Hager Commanded the Old Stone Fort in Schoharie, New York, in 1780.

Mr. Pelton is a member of Sons of the Revolution (SOR), and Sons of the American Revolution (SAR).

Please check my web site: `
www.robertwpelton.com

www.ingramcontent.com/pod-product-compliance
Lightning Source LLC
Chambersburg PA
CBHW070357290526
45790CB00004B/1535